Spanish for Little Girls

A beginning Spanish workbook
for little girls

Written by: Yvonne Crawford
Illustrated by: Angelique Lackey

www.languageforlittlelearners.com

Paudash Lake Publishing, 2011.
ISBN 978-0984454822

About this workbook

Most people learn a foreign language best when they are properly motivated. This workbook is designed to target the obsessions of little girls: princesses, tea parties, horses, and more. You and your daughter will open the door to the Spanish language while coloring flowers, playing memory games with different types of toys and hosting your own tea party in Spanish.

This workbook is created especially for parents who do not have any prior knowledge of Spanish. You and your daughter can embark on a journey of learning a foreign language together. Everything you need is inside this workbook, including a pronunciation guide, dictionary and teaching hints.

Every lesson will consist of a list of vocabulary words with pictures, three activities your daughter can do in the workbook with your guidance and two activities you can do together without the workbook for further practice. Each new word that is introduced will have its pronunciation next to it.

In the appendices there is a progress sheet for your child. When you and your child finish a lesson, turn to page 67 and have your child color a stepping stone. This will help your child to see, and take pride in her progress.

Try not to put stress on your daughter to have perfect pronunciation or to remember every single word. If she forgets a word, simply repeat it and then use it in a sentence a few times; eventually she will catch on. It is important for her (and you) to have a positive first experience with learning a foreign language. It will encourage her to continue in the future with more language studies.

If your daughter is learning quickly, have her try the challenges that are placed throughout the workbook. They are designed for children who need and desire more language learning.

Table of Contents

Lección 1

Hello Toys!

Vocabulary:

la muñeca
*lah-moo-**nyay**-kah*
doll

la cuerda de saltar
*lah-koo-**err**-dah-day-sal-**tahr***
jump rope

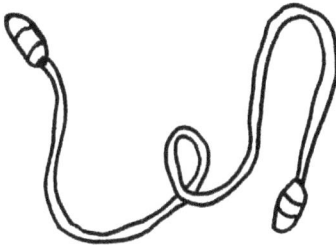

el juguete *ehl-hoo-**gay**-tay*
toy

el osito de peluche
*ehl-oh-**see**-toh-day-peh-**loo**-chay*
teddy bear

la casa de muñecas
*lah-**kah**-sah-day-moo-**nyay**-kahs*
doll house

Fun Phrases:

hola	**oh**-la	hello
adiós	a-dee-**ohs**	good-bye
hasta luego	**ahs**-tah-loo-**ay**-goh	see you later

Teaching Tips:

• Throughout the day, point out the bugs that you see and ask your child what they are called in Spanish. Before you know it your child will be making sentences like '¡Look, there's a *muñeca*!'

• Some letters sound different in Spanish than they do in English. Refer to each word's pronunciation guide to see the proper pronunciation.

• Usually for Spanish words which end in vowels, the stress is put on the 2nd to last syllable. If the word ends with a consonant, then the stress is put on the final syllable. In this workbook, the stressed syllable is bolded to aid teaching.

Actividad Uno

¡Hola! My name is Maria. I love to play games. Can you match the picture of each toy to its correct name?

la casa de muñecas

la muñeca

el osito de peluche

Actividad Dos

Now you can greet each of the toys in Spanish! For each picture above greet the toy, say '¡Hola!', then say the name of the toy.

Actividad Tres

Circle the toy that you like the most. Draw a line under the toy that you like the least. Draw a picture of your favorite *muñeca* in the box. Say *"adiós"* to each toy in this picture before you go to the next page.

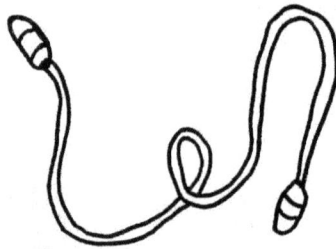

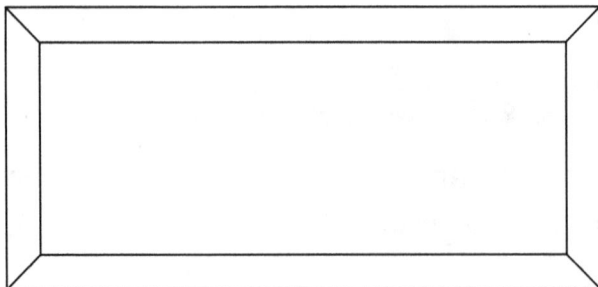

Actividad Cuatro

A Little Doll House

What you will need:

a box big enough to fit a doll inside
crayons
scissors
construction paper
tape or glue

What to do:

1. Take a box to create a doll house. Decorate your doll house with construction paper and crayons. You can even draw some decorations inside of the house. Make sure to get your mom or dad to help you cut out a door and some windows.
2. With your parent, play with your doll house and your dolls. Every time your dolls pass each other make sure you say 'hello' and good-bye' in Spanish.

Actividad Cinco

Rock Toys

What you will need:

a few flat rocks
paint
a paintbrush

What to do:

1. Paint each of the 5 toys listed in this lesson on the rocks. As you paint them make sure you repeat their names in Spanish.
2. After letting your rock toys dry, ask a parent to hide them in your backyard, sand pit, or anywhere. Then, as you find each toy, tell your parent which toy you found in Spanish.

Lección 2
Polite Pets

Maria's Pet Shop

el perro *ehl-**pehr**-roh*

el pez *ehl-**pays***
fish

el conejo
*ehl-coh-**nay**-hoh*
rabbit

el gato
*ehl-**gah**-toh*
cat

el pájaro
*ehl-**pah**-hah-roh*
bird

Fun Phrases:

¿Cómo estás?	*koh-moh-eh-stahs*	How are you?
estoy bien	*eh-stoy-bee-in*	I'm well.
estoy mal	*eh-stoy-mahl*	I'm bad.
así así	*ah-see-ah-see*	so-so
gracias	*grah-see-ahs*	thank you
de nada	*day-nah-dah*	you're welcome
por favor	*pohr-fay-vohr*	please

Teaching Tips:
• In Spanish when you say a sentence like, 'I'm well,' you do not need to say 'I'. Instead you drop 'I' (Yo).

Yo estoy bien —> Estoy bien.

• Encourage your child to color all of the vocabulary page pictures. You can use this time to reinforce the new words. You and your child can repeat each word as he colors its corresponding picture.

• Remember to watch for signs that your child needs to take a break. You can always start where you left off tomorrow!

• Unlike in English, in Spanish each sound is specifically spoken, so don't be afraid to really enunciate the sounds.

Actividad Uno

Come and meet my friends! Say ¡hola! to each animal. Next, draw a line from the animal to its favorite food. Your mom or dad can pretend to be the animal and say "*gracias*" for "thank you." You can reply "*de nada*" for "you're welcome" to each animal.

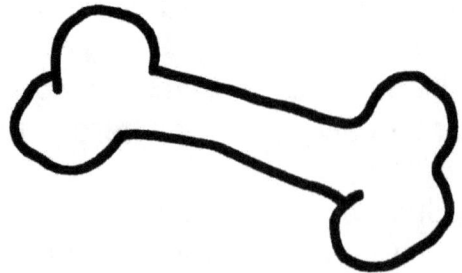

Actividad Dos

Oh no, the pets in the pictures have no mouths! Will you draw a mouth for each animal? Make two of the faces happy, one of the faces sad and one of the faces so-so. Then, when you are finished, ask the animal "*¿Cómo estás?*" Then, pretend to be the animal and reply with *Estoy bien*, *Estoy mal* or *así así*. Use the following rabbits as an example.

Actividad Tres

This is Maria's favorite story about her visit to a pet store to pick out a pet. Your mom or dad can read the story to you, and whenever you see a picture in the story, say the word in Spanish.

Maria	perro	conejo	gato	pez	pájaro

Maria's Trip to the Pet store

One day [Maria] decided that she wanted a pet. She asked her mom if she could have one. She said, "Okay [Maria], you may have one. Let's go to the pet store and pick one out." They went to the pet store and the first animal they saw was a big "[perro]. [Maria] jumped up and down and said "I want a "[perro]". Her mom replied "I'm sorry sweetie, a "[perro] is too big for our house, you need something smaller." She immediately found another pet that she liked, "Mom I would like this [pájaro], por favor." Her mother looked at the [pájaro] and imagined it tweeting all night. "I'm sorry, that [pájaro] is too loud, find a pet that is quieter." [Maria] looked and looked, then she saw a [conejo]. "I want this [conejo]. He's so quiet," [Maria] said.

16

Mom looked at the mess that the had made in his cage and she said "I'm sorry dear, he is too messy. You need to find a pet that is cleaner." saw a licking himself and she said, "A Mom? I think they are very clean." "Oh ", Mom said sadly, "I love cats, but the fur makes me sneeze, ah ah ah chooo!" was about to give up when she saw a swimming around in a bowl. She thought to herself, before she told her mom, The is not too big like a . It does not make too much noise, like a . It is not too messy, like a . It does not have fur that makes mom sneeze, like a . Maybe this pet might work. "Mom," asked tentatively, "Can I have a ? "Of course", mom replied. Maria and her mom went home with her new pet .

Fin - The End

Teaching Tips:

- You can repeat this story several times over the course of this book to reinforce the names of animals in Spanish.

Actividad Cuatro

Be Polite

Throughout the day, use your Spanish! When you would like something from your mom or dad, say "*por favor.*" The most important word is gra-cias for thank you. Also, there is *de nada* for you're welcome. Every time you say one of these polite expressions today, you can come back to this workbook and record it on this page. Color a star for each time you use one of your new Spanish phrases.

por favor   *gracias*   *de nada*

☆ ☆ ☆ ☆ ☆ ☆ ☆ ☆ ☆

Actividad Cinco

Faces

What you will need:
construction paper
markers/crayons
scissors

What to do:
1. With your mom's or dad's help, cut out three big circles.
2. Draw a face in each circle. Make sure to include eyes, a nose, ears, and hair on each of the three circles.
3. Now, draw a smiley mouth on one circle, a frown on one circle and a so-so face on the last circle. As you are drawing the mouths, repeat the phrases in Spanish "*estoy bien,*" "*estoy mal*" and "*así así.*"
4. Take a large piece of construction paper, tape all of the faces onto it, and hang it on the fridge.
5. Throughout the day, go to the faces and practice saying "How are you?" in Spanish by saying "*¿Cómo estás?,*" then you can point to the face that shows how you feel, and say the phrase in Spanish.

Lección 3

Growing with Numbers

Vocabulary:

la flor *lah-flohr*
flower

la rosa *lah-roh-sah*
rose

el árbol
ehl-ahr-bohl
tree

el jardín
ehl-hahr-deen
garden

la hoja
lah-oh-hah
leaf

1 **uno** *oo-noh*
one

2 **dos** *dohs*
two

3 **tres** *trays*
three

4 **cuatro** *koo-**aht**-troh*
four

5 **cinco** *seen-koh*
five

Teaching Tips:

- In order to reinforce learning the numbers, use the Spanish numbers throughout the day.   Whenever your child says a number in English, ask them to say it in Spanish as well.

- When a word ends with a vowel, add an 's' to the end of a noun to make it plural.

una rosa - one rose
dos rosas - two roses

Actividad Uno

Count the different flowers in Spanish, then write the number in the box.

Actividad Dos

This beautiful *flor* needs some petals. Circle the group with *cuatro* petals. Then, draw the petals on the flower.

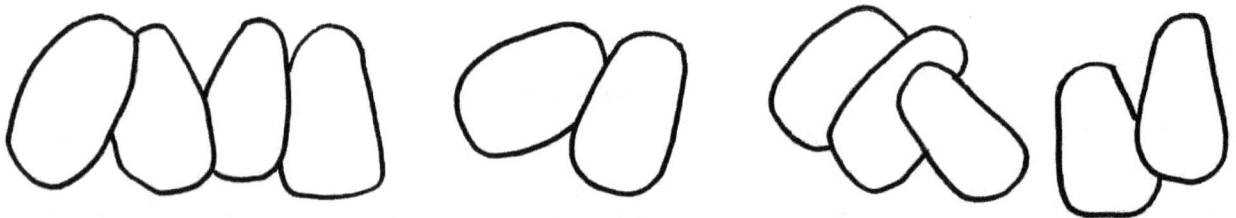

Challenge:

Take a few toasted oat cereal rings and make a flower out of them. Put one in the middle and then put a few around as the petals. Count the number of "petals" on each flower you make in Spanish.

Actividad Tres

Follow the path of each falling *hoja* and find out which one leads to me!

Actividad Cuatro

Counting Flowers

Go outside and gather five flowers or leaves, then count them. Say phrases like: *cinco flores* and *dos hojas*. You can also practice being polite by sharing your flowers and leaves with your parents. When you give them a flower or leaf, they can say *gracias* and you can reply *de nada*.

Actividad Cinco

Garden Scrapbook

What you will need:

flowers and leaves (you can either use fresh or dry them)
construction paper
glue
scissors
a hole punch
yarn
crayons

What to do:

1. Walk around your backyard or a park and pick a few flowers and leaves that you like. (Ask you mom to make sure it's okay to pick a few flowers.)
2. Repeat their names in Spanish as you pick them.
3. Fold a piece of construction paper in half and glue your flowers and leaves on all parts of the paper. You can pick the petals off of the flower so that it will be easier to glue them.
4. After you finish gluing leaves and flowers to your scrapbook, have your parents help you punch holes in it on one side, thread a piece of yarn through the holes, and then tie the yarn in order to bind your book.
5. Finally, decorate your book by coloring it. You can also ask your parents to help you write the names of the leaves and flowers in Spanish in your scrapbook.

Lección 4

Colors

Vocabulary:

verde *vehrr-day*
green

azul *ah-sool*
blue

rojo *roh-hoh*
red

amarillo *ah-mah-ree-yoh*
yellow

negro *nay-groh*
black

blanco *blahn-koh*
white

anaranjado *ah-nah-rahn-hah-doh*
orange

Fun Phrases:

me llamo	*meh-**yah**-moh*	my name is
¿Cómo te llamas?	***koh**-moh-tay-**yah**-mahs*	what is your name?
y	*ee*	and
la sirena	*lah-see-**ray**-nah*	mermaid

Teaching tips:
- Most adjectives in Spanish follow the noun, for example:
    la sirena azul - the blue mermaid
    la sirena verde - the green mermaid

Challenge:
- You can also ask this question to your child to reinforce colors.
    ¿Cuál color? *koo-**ahl**-koo-**lohr*** - which color?

Actividad Uno

Let's color my animal friends. Use the key to color the different animals.

el pájaro	verde
el perro	azul
el gato	anaranjado
el pez	negro
el conejo	amarillo

Actividad Dos

Color the items in the garden below in different colors and say their names in Spanish.

Challenge:

Use *hay (**ah**-ee)* which means "there is/there are" to explain to your parents what is happening in this picture.

Hay una flor roja. - There is a red flower.

Actividad Tres

Use the frame below and draw a picture of yourself. Write your name at the bottom after *Me llamo* and show your mom and dad that you can say "My name is…" in Spanish.

Me llamo _____.

Actividad Cuatro

Rainbow Rice

What you will need:

rice
food coloring
a plastic container with a lid

What to do:

1. Take the bag of rice and pour it into the plastic container
2. Spread the rice evenly in the container.
3. Pick up each bottle of food coloring, and practice saying the names of the colors in Spanish.
4. With your mom or dad's help, pour the different colors of food coloring into separate sections of the rice. Try not to mix them up so that you will have nice vibrant colors.
5. Allow the rice to dry for at least 1 hour.
6. Now, you can play with your special new colored rice. As you play you can talk about the different colors. Have fun with it!

Actividad Cinco

Hello Friends

What you will need:

Your favorite toys with names (if they don't have names, now may be the time to name them) - dolls, stuffed animals, anything…

What to do:

1. Line up all of your toys and ask the first toy *"¿Cómo te llamas?"* which means "What is your name?"
2. Then, reply for your toy (in a different voice) *"Me llamo…"*
3. Continue with the rest of your toys doing the same thing.

Lección 5
More Magical Numbers

Vocabulary:

el unicornio
*ehl-oo-nee-**kohr**-nee-oh*
unicorn

el castillo *ehl-kahs-**tee**-yoh*
castle

la corona
*lah-koh-**roh**-nah*
crown

la reina *lah-**ray**-nah*
queen

el pegaso
*ehl-pay-**gah**-soh*
pegasus

seis *say-ees* **6**
six

siete *see-**eh**-tay* **7**
seven

ocho *oh-choh* **8**
eight

nueve *noo-**ay**-vay* **9**
nine

diez *dee-**ehs*** **10**
ten

30

Actividad Uno

¡Hola! Look at the picture below. Can you help me find all of the magical things? Each time you find one, use your Spanish. Say "I see a …" or "*Veo…*" When you find one, color it! And at the end you can count all of the magical things that you have colored!

Actividad Dos

Maria has drawn a picture for you, but she has forgotten to connect some of the dots. Use your crayon and connect all of the dots to finish his picture. As you connect the dots say each number in Spanish!

5

3

7

1

2

4

6

8

9

0

10

Actividad Tres

Count the pictures below in Spanish, and then circle the correct number.

5	6	7

8	10	9

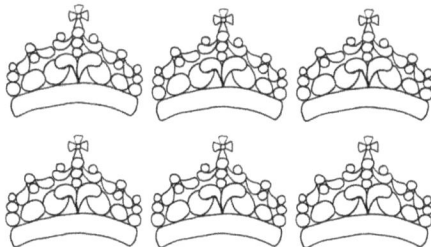

7	6	5

7	9	8

Challenge:

Start a collection of objects! Brainstorm with your parent about different things that could be in your collection (dolls, sea shells, pencils, stamps, postcards). After gathering the objects for your collection, count the number of items in your collection in Spanish.

Actividad Cuatro

Your Crown

What you will need:

constuction paper
glitter
crayons or markers
tape or glue
scissors
yarn

What to do:

1. Imagine you are a queen. What kind of crown would you like to wear?
2. Using all of the supplies, create a crown from your imagination.
3. After you have completed your crown you can wear it by attaching a piece of yarn.

Actividad Cinco

A Magestic Scepter

What you will need:

empty paper towel roll
construction paper
crayons
yarn
scissors
tape or glue

What to do:

1. Using one piece of construction paper, roll it around the roll.
2. Decorate your scepter by coloring diamonds and hearts on it.
3. Cut pieces of yarn to hang down from your scepter.
4. Cut small pieces of construction paper to hang down from the yarn.
5. Cut out a big star for the top of the scepter.
6. After your scepter is complete you can use it with your *corona* and pretend to be a *reina*.

Lección 6

Pretty Princesses

Vocabulary:

la princesa
lah-prin-say-sah
princess

la cabeza
lah-kah-bay-sah
head

el brazo
ehl-brah-soh
arm

el dedo *ehl-day-doh*
finger

la mano
lah-mah-noh
hand

la pierna *lah-pee-ehr-nah*
leg

le pie *ehl-pee-ay*
foot

el dedo *ehl-day-doh*
toe

Fun Phrases:

tengo	*tayn*-goh	I have
tienes	tee-*ehn*-ehs	you have

Teaching Tips:

- It's important to review previous lessons to make sure your child remembers other words she has learned.

Challenge:

- Use this question word to help your child practice numbers in Spanish:

cuántos	**quahn**-tohs	how many

Actividad Uno

Let's design a princess! Below are the bodies and heads of two princesses, use your crayons to draw *piernas, manos, dedos,* and all other parts of the princess like her crown and scepter. As you draw each body part, say the word in Spanish.

Actividad Dos

Look at the different pictures of princesses. In each row find
the one princess that is different from the other two and tell your parent
which part is different. Then, tell your parent the different body parts in
Spanish.

Actividad Tres

Say these words in Spanish and then draw a line from each word to its matching picture.

la pierna   **el brazo**   **el dedo**   **la cabeza**

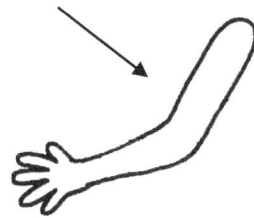

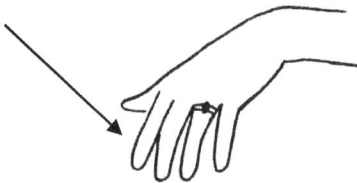

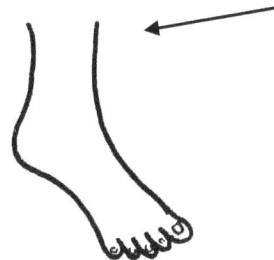

Challenge:

Sing and act out the "Hokey Pokey" song with your child using the Spanish term for each body part focus on in this lesson. You can sing the song in English and say the body parts in Spanish. For example: "You put your right *pierna* in. You put your right *pierna* out. You put your right *pierna* in and you shake it all about. You do the hokey pokey and you turn yourself around. That's what it's all about!"

Actividad Cuatro

Making Princesses

What you will need:

Modeling clay

What to do:

1. Make princess body parts together with your mom or dad. As you finish making each body part say the name and color of it in Spanish. For example: *la cabeza roja*
2. Build some princesses. After you have built a few princesses, you can pretend to be a princess and speak to your mom or dad. You can say things like "*¡Hola!*" and "*¿Cómo estás?*"

Challenge:

You can also describe what you see:

veo	**vay**-oh	I see

Veo una pierna roja. I see a red leg.

Actividad Cinco

A Paper Me

What you will need:

freezer paper
crayons
scissors

What to do:

1. Roll out a big sheet of freezer paper on the floor - about the size of yourself.
2. Have your mom or dad trace your body onto the paper.
3. Draw and color your hair, face and clothes.
4. Ask your mom or dad to help cut out your picture of yourself and then hang it on a wall or door.
5. Point to all of your body parts on the picture and say their names in Spanish.

Lección 7

Let's Go Horseback Riding

Vocabulary:

el caballo *ehl-kah-**bah**-yoh*
horse

el poni *ehl-**poh**-nee*
pony

la vaquera lah-vah-**kay**-rah
cowgirl

la jinete
*lah-hee-**nay**-tay*
horseback rider (girl)

las botas *lahs-**boh**-tahs*
boots

el sombrero *ehl-sohm-**bray**-roh*
hat

Fun Phrases:

aquí	ah-**kee**	here
allí	ah-**yee**	there
veo	**vay**-oh	I see
ves	vays	you see

Challenge:
• If your child is ready, you can teach her how to form a question in Spanish. Simply change the intonation of your voice. Below are some examples:

Ves una vaquera. You see a cowgirl.

¿Ves una vaquera? Do you see a cowgirl?

Hay dos botas. There are 2 boots.

¿Hay dos botas? Are there 2 boots?

• Remember to teach these lessons as slowly or as quickly as your child needs. If your child is not ready for this challenge, you can always come back to it at a later time.

Actividad Uno

Uh oh, this cowgirl is trying to find her cow. Follow the maze until she finds her cow. You can use a different color crayon for each path you try. Remember to say the name of the color you are using.

Actividad Dos

What do all cowgirls wear? What do you wear when you dress up as a cowgirl? Help make the little girl below to become a cowgirl. As you draw the items she needs, say their names in Spanish.

Actividad Tres

Hmmmm...a few things are just a bit different, but what? Find the nine differences between the two pictures below. Count the differences in Spanish.

Actividad Cuatro

Make Your horse

What you will need:

shoe box
construction paper
crayons or markers
glue or tape
scissors
string/yarn

What to do:

1. Tape the lid onto the top of the shoe box.
2. Use your imagination and decorate the shoe box to make it look like a horse. Make sure to put a saddle on top.
3. Now, you need to take your new horse on a delivery trip. Find things you have that you can deliver to your mom or dad. You can tell them what the colors of the items are in Spanish, when you deliver them.

Actividad Cinco

Toys

What you will need:

Some of your toys, dolls, stuffed animals, etc. (Use can use anything that we have learned the name of in a previous lesson.)

What to do:

1. Sit down with your mom and dad to play this game.
2. She will say in *Tengo*….and then select 1 toy. Then you say *Tienes...* and then the name of the toy.
3. Continue until you both have named all of your toys.

For example:
Your mom might say: *Tengo un osito de peluche.*
You would reply: *Tienes un osito de peluche.*

Lección 8
A Day at the Zoo

Vocabulary:

león *ehl-lay-**ohn***
lion

el elefante
*ehl-ay-lay-**fahn**-tay*
elephant

el oso *ehl-**oh**-soh*
bear

la jirafa *lah-hee-**rah**-fah*
giraffe

cebra *lah-**say**-brah*
zebra

el tigre *ehl-**tee**-gray*
tiger

el parque zoológico *ehl-**pahr**-keh-zoh-**loh**-hee-koh*

ZOO

Fun Phrases:

pequeño	pay-**kay**-nyoh	small
grande	**grahn**-day	big
lento	**lehn**-toh	slow
rápido	**rah**-pee-doh	fast
soy	soy	I am
eres	**eh**-rehs	you are

Teaching Tips:

- As you have learned, most adjectives in Spanish go after the noun; however, some adjectives in Spanish go before the noun, such as *pequeño* and *grande*.

el pequeño gato - the little cat

Actividad Uno

Oh no! The animals have escaped from their pens! Can you draw a line between the animals and their correct pens? Remember to say the animal's name in Spanish as you draw the line.

la cebra

el oso

el elefante

Actividad Dos

Look at all of the different animals on this page. Some are *grande* and some are very *pequeño*. Using your crayons or markers, draw a *rojo* circle around all of the *grande* animals. Draw a *verde* circle around all of the *pequeño* animals.

Actividad Tres

Uh oh...the animals are all mixed up! Look at each picture and say which parts of each animal make up this new animal. In the empty box, create your own mixed up animal. Then, describe all of the mixed up animals to your parents in Spanish. Remember to use the names of the body parts you have learned!

Actividad Cuatro

Animal Parade

What you will need:

paper plates
crayons
scissors
construction paper
glue

What to do:

1. Create your own animal mask by using the materials listed. You can also make a tail for yourself.
2. Have an animal parade around your house. Make sure you say
   Soy (I am)... (I am) to let everyone know which animal you are.
   For example: *Soy un tigre.* (I am a tiger.)

Actividad Cinco

Animal Charades

What you will need:

strips of paper
a cup
a pencil

What to do:

1. Ask your mom or dad to write the names or draw pictures of the animals from this chapter on strips of paper.
2. Fold up the strips of paper and put them in the cup.
3. Take turns with your mom or dad taking a piece of paper from the cup and pretending to be that animal. Try not to make sounds or use words when acting out your animal. Make sure to guess the animal name in Spanish.

Lección 9
Sugar, Spice and Everything Yummy

Vocabulary:

la galleta *lah-gah-yeh-tah*
cookie

el pastel *ehl-pahs-tehl*
cake

el helado *ehl-lah-doh*
ice cream

el dulce *ehl-dool-say*
candy

la tarta *lah-tahr-tah*
pie

Fun Phrases:

me gusta	meh-**goo**-stah	I like
te gusta	teh-**goo**-stah	you like

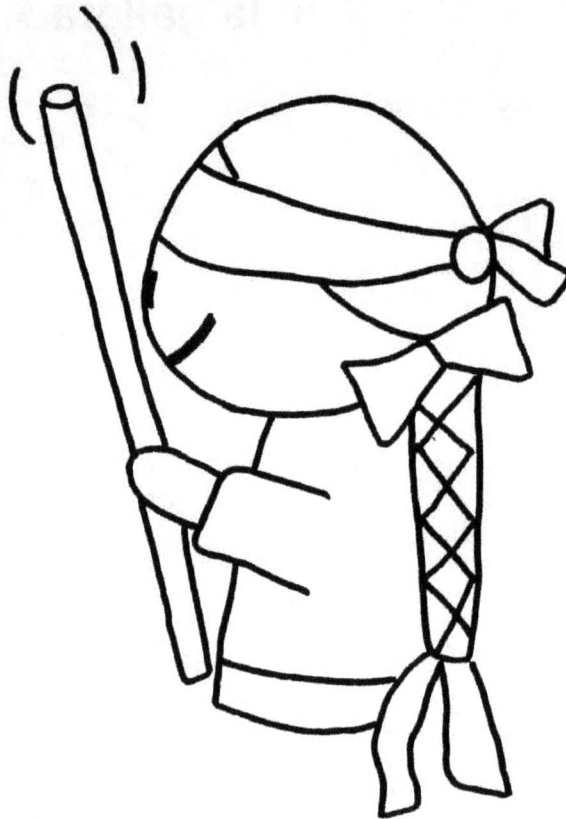

Challenge:

You can have your daughter practice saying things she likes with plural nouns. If a noun is either masculine or both masculine and feminine the plural for 'the' is los and las if the noun is feminine. Also, if a word ends with a consonant sound, you need to add 'es' to the end of the word to make it plural.

She can practice phrases like:

      Me gustan las galletas. I love the cookies
      Me gustan los dulces. I love the candy.

Actividad Uno

Maria has baked all sorts of goodies. Match the pairs by drawing a line to the matching pictures and say their names in Spanish.

Actividad Dos

Ladders and Ribbons

What you will need:

a die

a counter for each player, for example a small plastic animal or toy car

Vocabulary:

comienzo	*koh-mee-**ehn**-soh*	start
fin	*feen*	end

	9	**10**
	8	**7**
comienzo	**1**	**2**

How to Play:

1. The youngest person goes first. Roll the die and then move that many spaces. Count in Spanish as you move your counter.
2. If you land on a ribbon, you have to slide down it and land on the square at the bottom of it.
3. If you land on a ladder, you can climb up to the square it ends on.
4. The first person to reach the finish (*fin*) is the winner!

¡Buena suerte! Good luck!

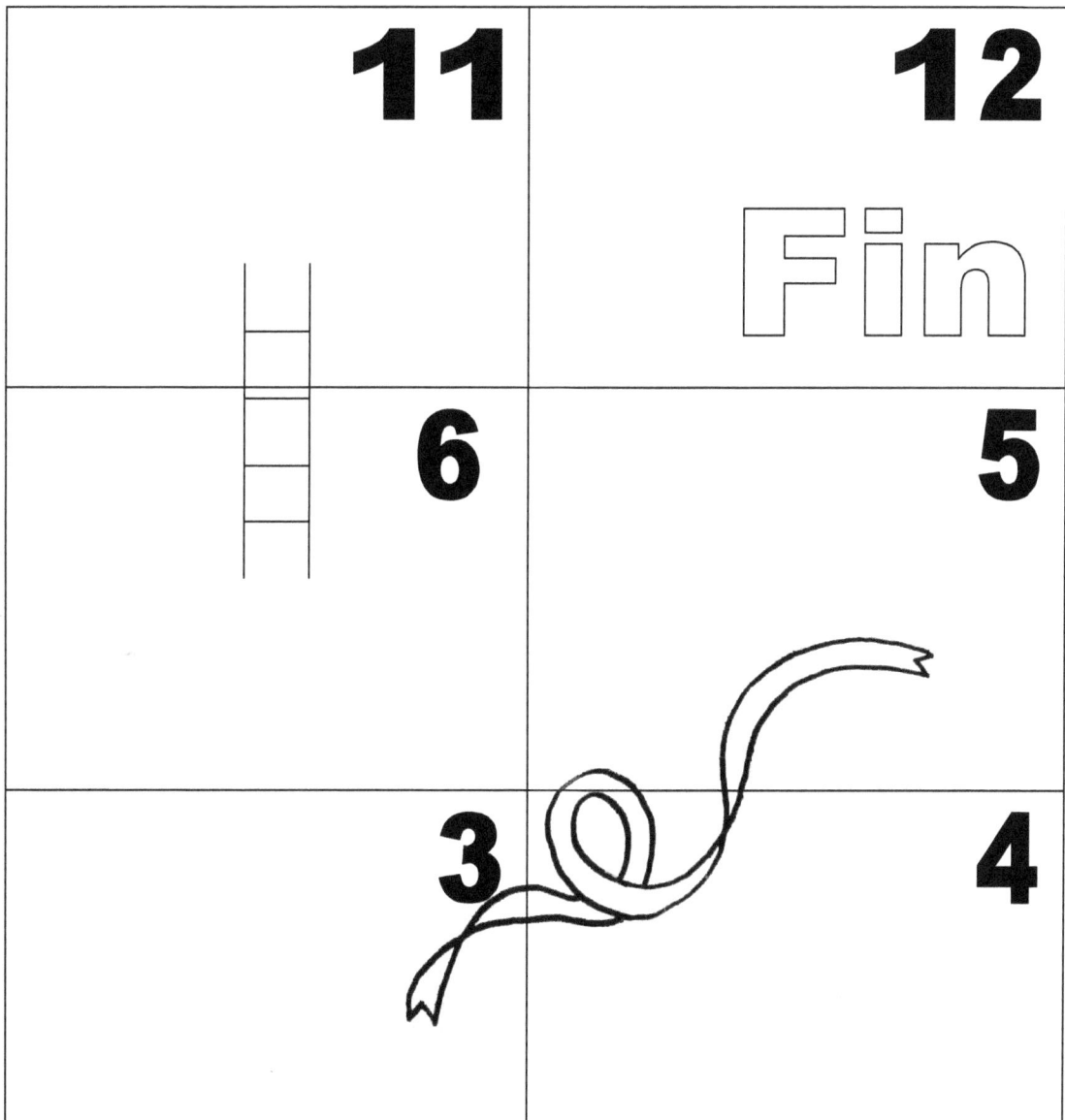

11	**12** Fin
6	**5**
3	**4**

Actividad Tres

Maria, wants to go home. As she passes friends on the road, say in Spanish each animal's name and the other things she sees. Say *veo*…Then, color the picture using the color key below.

color key	
el gato	negro
el tigre	anaranjado
el perro	rojo
la cebra	verde
el poni	azul

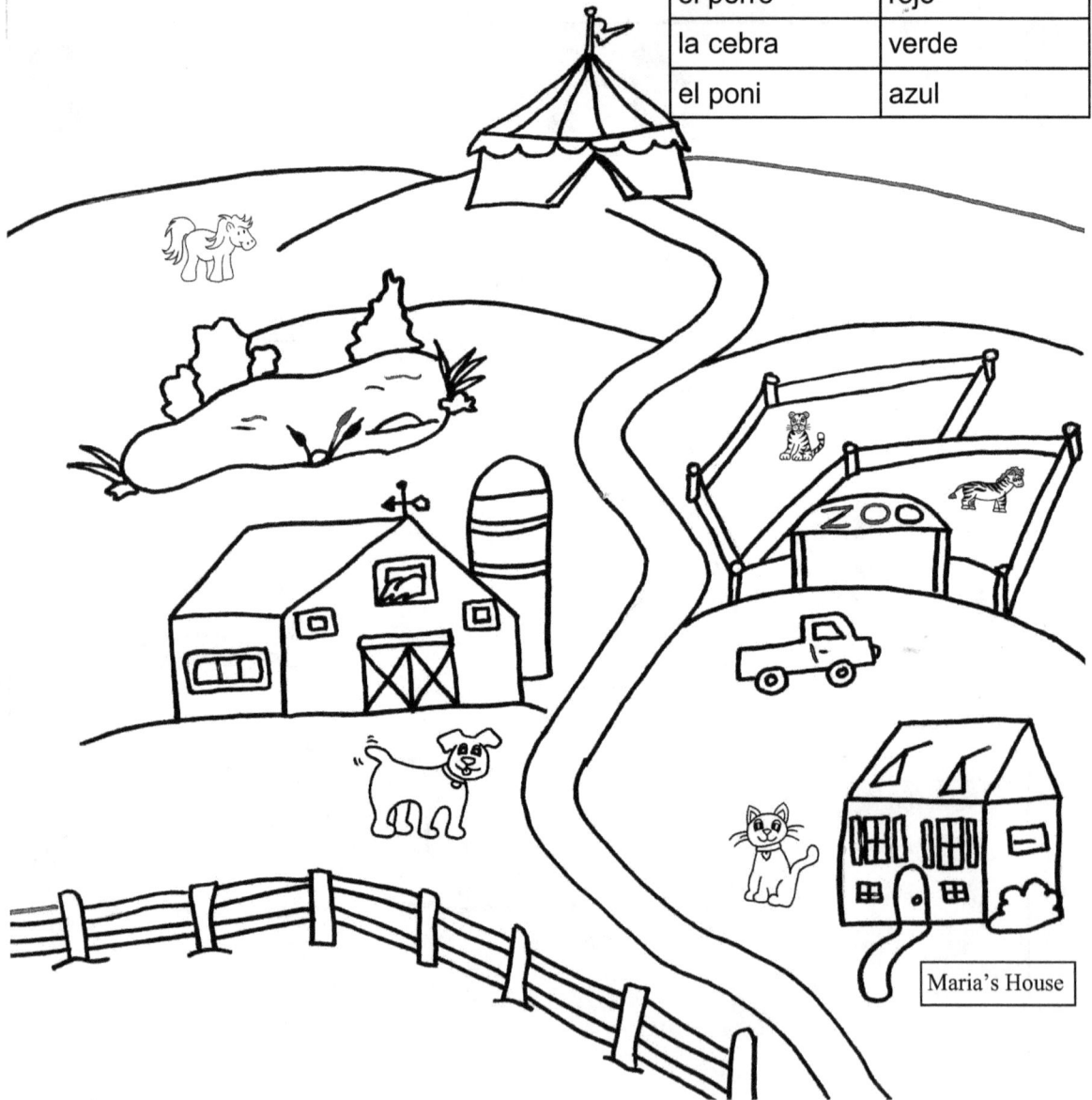

Maria's House

Actividad Cuatro

Making cookies

What you will need:

cotton balls
acrylic paint
scissors
paper
glue

What to do:

1. Have your mom or dad help you draw and cut the shape of different cookies out of paper.
2. Dip your cotton balls into different colors of paint and let them dry.
3. Glue your cotton balls onto the paper and create very colorful cookies. After you let them dry, you can hang them on your fridge. Every time you go to the fridge, point to the different colors and say their names in Spanish.

Actividad Cinco

I Like...

What you will need:

construction paper
crayons

What to do:

1. Take a piece of construction paper and at the top write *me gusta* on it. You can ask your mom or dad to help you.
2. Draw all of the things that *te gusta*. They could be people, toys, places; anything that *te gusta*.
3. Show your mom and dad your artwork and tell them all of the things that *te gusta*.

Lección 10

Tea Time

Vocabulary:

la taza de té
*lah-**tahs**-sah-day-tee*
tea cup

la tetera *lah-tay-**tay**-rah*
tea pot

la merienda *lah-may-ree-**ehn**-dah*
tea time

el plato *ehl-**plah**-toh*
plate

Challenge:
- To create a negative sentence in Spanish, put 'no' before the verb.
For example:

I don't see the plate.
No veo el plato.

Actividad Uno

Color my friend according to the key below. As you color the picture, make sure you say the colors' names and numbers in Spanish.

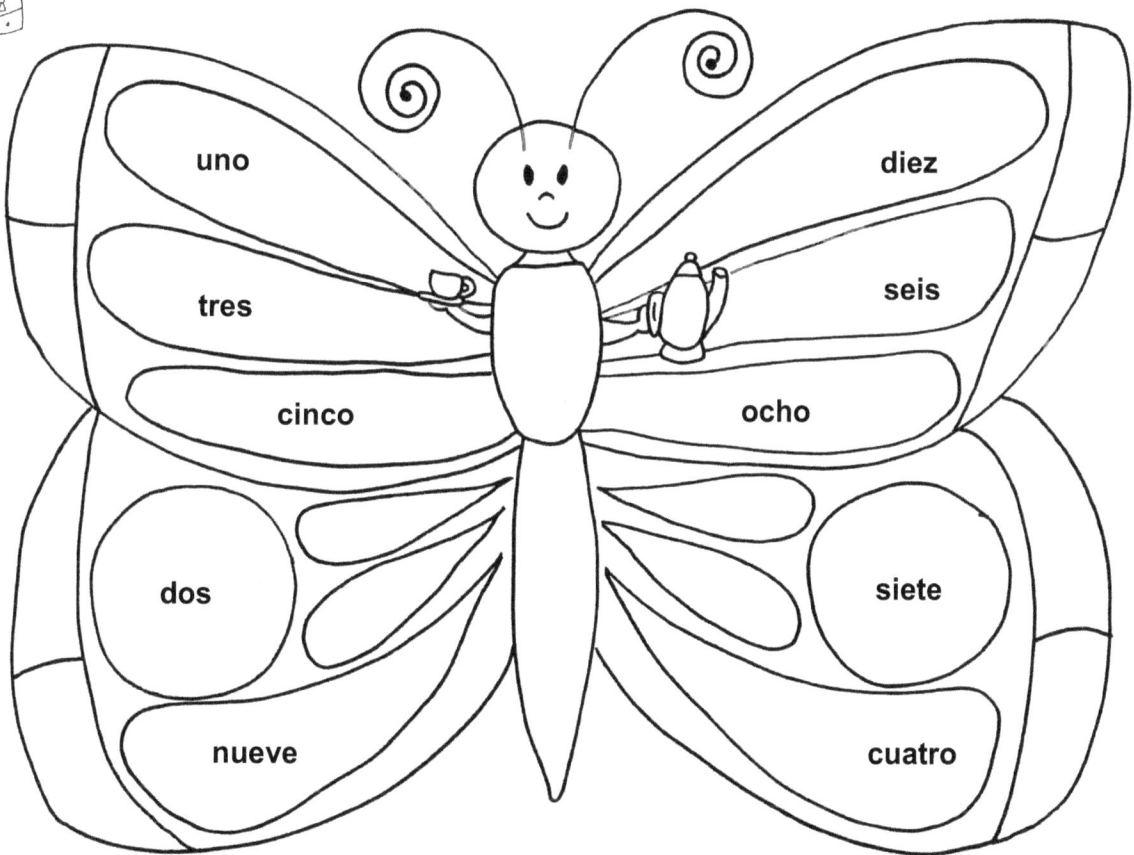

uno

diez

tres

seis

cinco

ocho

dos

siete

nueve

cuatro

un	verde
dos	azul
tres	anaranjado
cuatro	negro
cinco	rojo

seis	blanco
siete	amarillo
ocho	rojo
nueve	verde
diez	azul

Actividad Dos

Maria is getting ready for a tea party. She wants you to count the hearts on each tea cup in Spanish and write the number below the cup.

Actividad Tres

Maria needs your help to find her way to the *galleta*. As you pass a number, make sure to say that number in Spanish.

Actividad Cuatro

Memory

You will need:
the memory cards found in the appendix of this book.

What to do:
1. Shuffle the cards.
2. Turn all of the cards upside down in rows in front of you on a table or on the floor.
3. Pick up 2 and see if they match. As you pick up each card, remember to say each picture's name in Spanish. If they match, you can keep those cards and continue with your turn. If they do not match, put them back upside-down and then it will be the next player's turn.
4. The player with the most pairs of matched cards wins.

Challenge: You can vary the level of difficulty of this game by using some or all of the pairs of cards.

Actividad Cinco

Tea Party

You will need:
toy dishes
some cookies/treats
milk

What to do:
1. Set the table with your toy dishes to get ready for a Spanish tea party.
2. Put out cookies, treats, and milk.
3. Invite your mother, father or siblings to the tea party. Practice all of the phrases you've learned in this book. Say *hola* when they first come to your tea party and adiós when they leave.

Change it up: Instead of using real cookies, use the cookies you made in the previous lesson. This way you can practice your colors as well.

Appendices

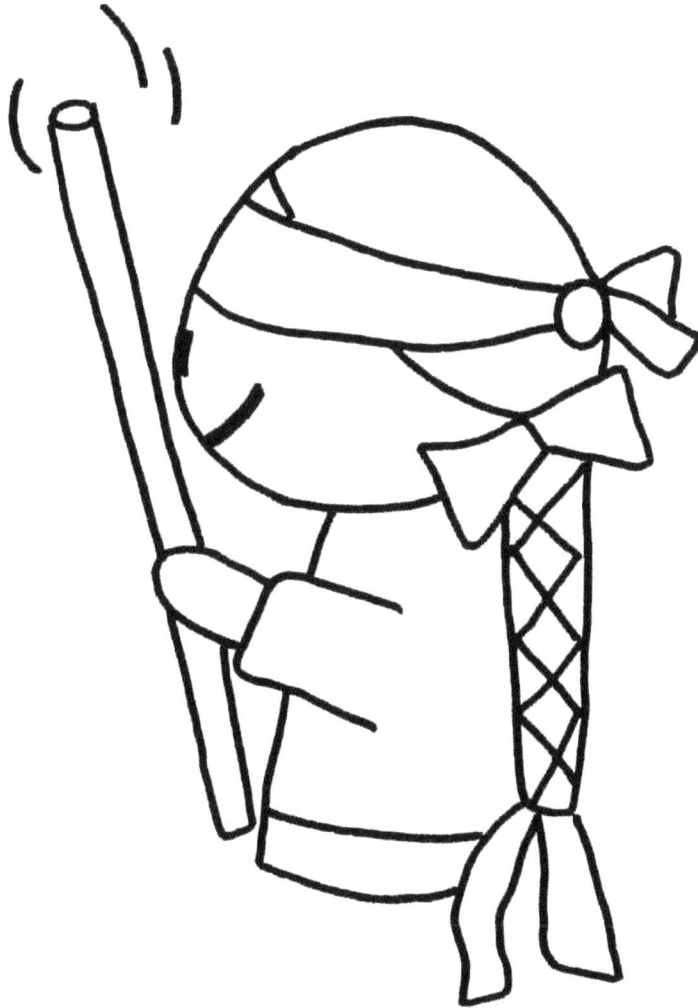

My Spanish Path

Every time you finish a *lección* in the book,
color a stone until you reach Maria.

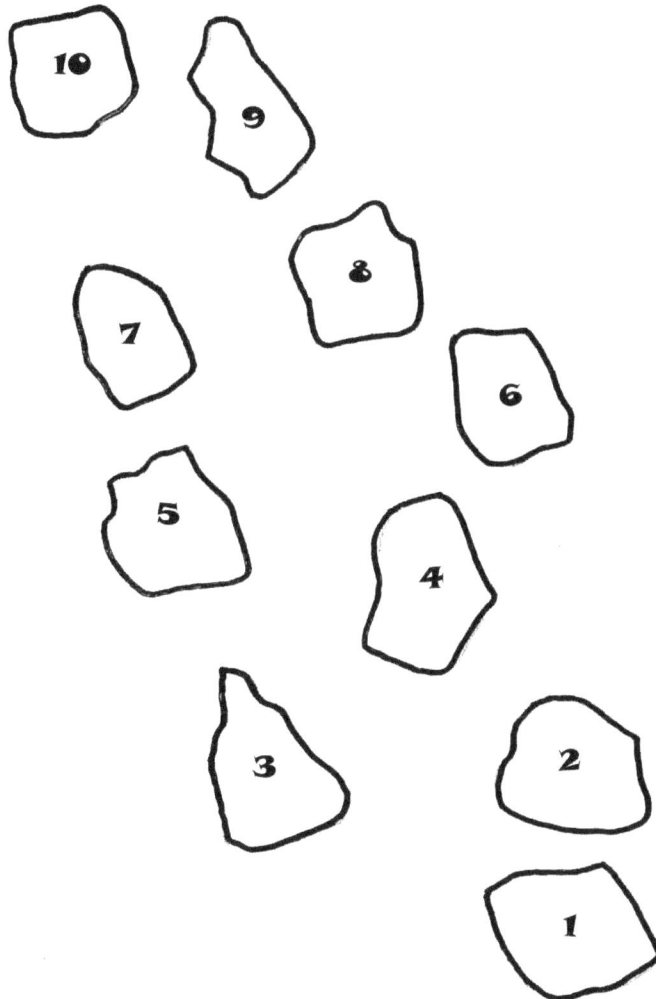

10

9

8

7

6

5

4

3

2

1

Three cheers for

¡Felicidades!
Congratulations!
You have successfully finished
Spanish for Little Girls.
You did a wonderful job!

English to Spanish Dictionary

a(n)	un/una	*oohn/**ooh**-nah*
and	y	*ee*
arm	**el brazo**	*ehl-**brah**-soh*
bear	**el oso**	*ehl-**oh**-soh*
big	**grande**	***grahn**-day*
bird	**el pájaro**	*ehl-**pah**-hah-roh*
black	**negro**	***nay**-groh*
blue	**azul**	*ah-**sool***
boots	**las botas**	*lahs-**boh**-tahs*
cake	**el pastel**	*ehl-pahs-**tehl***
candy	**el dulce**	*ehl-**dool**-say*
castle	**el castillo**	*ehl-kahs-**tee**-yoh*
cat	**el gato**	*ehl-**gah**-toh*

color	el color	*ehl-koo-**lohr***
congratulations	felicidades	*feh-lee-cee-**dah**-days*
cookie	la galleta	*lah-gah-**yeh**-tah*
cowgirl	la vaquera	*lah-vah-**kay**-rah*
crown	la corona	*lah-koh-**roh**-nah*
dog	el perro	*ehl-**pehr**-roh*
doll	la muñeca	*lah-moo-**nyay**-kah*
doll house	la casa de muñecas	*lah-**kah**-sah-day-moo-**nyay**-kahs*
eight	ocho	***oh**-choh*
elephant	el elefante	*ehl-ay-lay-**fahn**-tay*
end	fin	*feen*
fast	rápido	***rah**-pee-doh*
finger	el dedo	*ehl-**day**-doh*
fish	el pez	*ehl-pays*

five	cinco	*seen*-koh
flower	la flor	*lah-flohr*
foot	le pie	*ehl-pee-ay*
four	cuatro	*koo-aht-troh*
garden	el jardín	*ehl-hahr-deen*
giraffe	la jirafa	*lah-hee-rah-fah*
good-bye	adiós	*a-dee-ohs*
good luck	buena suerte	*boo-eh-nah-swehr-teh*
green	verde	*vehrr-day*
hand	la mano	*lah-mah-noh*
hat	el sombrero	*ehl-sohm-bray-roh*
have a good trip	que tengas un buen viaje	*key-tehn-gahs-oohn-booehn-vee-ah-hay*
head	la cabeza	*lah-kah-bay-sah*
hello	hola	*oh-la*

here	aquí	*ah-**kee***
horse	el caballo	*ehl-kah-**bah**-yoh*
horseback rider	la jinete	*lah-hee-**nay**-tay*
how are you?	¿cómo estás?	***koh**-moh-eh-**stahs***
how many?	cuántos	***quahn**-tohs*
I am	soy	*soy*
I have	tengo	***tayn**-goh*
I like	me gusta	*meh-**goo**-stah*
I see	veo	***vay**-oh*
ice cream	el helado	*ehl-**lah**-doh*
it's going poorly	estoy mal	*eh-**stoy**-mahl*
it's going well	estoy bien	*eh-**stoy**-bee-**in***
jump rope	la cuerda de sal-tar	*lah-koo-**err**-dah-day-sal-tahr*

leaf	la hoja	*lah-**oh**-hah*
leg	la pierna	*lah-pee-**ehr**-nah*
lesson	la lección	*la-lek-see-**ohn***
lion	el león	*ehl-lay-**ohn***
mermaid	la sirena	*lah-see-**ray**-nah*
my name is	me llamo	*meh-**yah**-moh*
nine	nueve	*noo-**ay**-vay*
no	no	*noh*
one	uno	***oo**-noh*
orange	anaranjado	*ah-nah-rahn-**hah**-doh*
pegasus	el pegaso	*ehl-pay-**gah**-soh*
pie	la tarta	*lah-**tahr**-tah*
plate	el plato	*ehl-**plah**-toh*
please	por favor	*pohr-fay-**vohr***

pony	el poni	*ehl-**poh**-nee*
princess	la princesa	lah-prin-**say**-sah
queen	la reina	lah-**ray**-nah
rabbit	el conejo	*ehl-coh-**nay**-hoh*
red	rojo	***roh**-hoh*
rose	la rosa	*lah-**roh**-sah*
see you later	hasta luego	***ahs**-tah-loo-**ay**-goh*
seven	siete	*see-**eh**-tay*
six	seis	***say**-ees*
slow	lento	***lehn**-toh*
small	pequeño	*pay-**kay**-nyoh*
so-so	así así	*ah-**see**-ah-**see***
start	comienzo	*koh-mee-**ehn**-so*
tea cup	la taza de té	*lah-**tahs**-sah-day-tee*

tea time	la merienda	*lah-may-ree-**ehn**-dah*
tea pot	la tetera	*lah-tay-**tay**-rah*
teddy bear	el osito de peluche	*ehl-oh-**see**-toh-day-peh-**loo**-chay*
ten	diez	*dee-**ehs***
thank you	gracias	**grah**-see-ahs
there	allí	*ah-**yee***
there is/there are	hay	*ah-ee*
three	tres	*trays*
tiger	el tigre	*ehl-**tee**-gray*
toe	el dedo	*ehl-**day**-doh*
toy	el juguete	*ehl-hoo-**gay**-tay*
tree	el árbol	*ehl-**ahr**-bohl*
two	dos	*dohs*
unicorn	el unicornio	*ehl-oo-nee-**kohr**-nee-oh*

what is you name?	¿cómo te lla-mas?	**koh**-moh-tay-**yah**-mahs
which	cuál	koo-**ahl**
white	blanco	**blahn**-koh
yellow	amarillo	ah-mah-**ree**-yoh
you are	eres	**eh**-rehs
you're welcome	de nada	day-**nah**-dah
you have	tienes	tee-**ehn**-ehs
you like	tu gusta	teh-**goo**-stah
you see	ves	vays
zebra	la cebra	lah-**say**-brah
zoo	el parque **zoo**-lógico	ehl-**pahr**-keh-zoh-**loh**-hee-koh

Spanish to English Dictionary

adiós	*a-dee-**ohs***	good-bye
allí	*ah-**yee***	there
amarillo	*ah-mah-**ree**-yoh*	yellow
anaranjado	*ah-nah-rahn-**hah**-doh*	orange
aquí	*ah-**kee***	here
el árbol	*ehl-**ahr**-bohl*	tree
así así	*ah-**see**-ah-**see***	so-so
azul	*ah-**sool***	blue
blanco	***blahn**-koh*	white
las botas	*lahs-**boh**-tahs*	boots
el brazo	*ehl-**brah**-soh*	arm
buena suerte	*boo-**eh**-nah-**swehr**-teh*	good luck
la cabeza	*lah-kah-**bay**-sah*	head

la casa de muñecas	lah-**kah**-sah-day-moo-**nyay**-kahs	doll house
el castillo	ehl-kahs-**tee**-yoh	castle
la cebra	lah-**say**-brah	zebra
cinco	**seen**-koh	five
el color	ehl-koo-**lohr**	color
comienzo	koh-mee-**ehn**-soh	start
¿cómo estás?	**koh**-moh-eh-**stahs**	how are you?
¿cómo te lla-mas?	**koh**-moh-tay-**yah**-mahs	What is your name?
el conejo	ehl-coh-**nay**-hoh	rabbit
la corona	lah-koh-**roh**-nah	crown
cuál	koo-**ahl**	which
cuántos	**quahn**-tohs	how many?
cuatro	koo-**aht**-troh	four
el dedo	ehl-**day**-doh	finger/toe

diez	*dee-**ehs***	ten
dos	*dohs*	two
el dulce	*ehl-**dool**-say*	candy
el elefante	*ehl-ay-lay-**fahn**-tay*	elephant
eres	***eh**-rehs*	you are
estoy bien	*eh-**stoy**-bee-in*	I'm well
estoy mal	*eh-**stoy**-mahl*	I'm bad
felicidades	*feh-lee-cee-**dah**-days*	congratulations
fin	*feen*	end
la flor	*lah-flohr*	flower
la galleta	*lah-gah-**yeh**-tah*	cookie
el gato	*ehl-**gah**-toh*	cat
gracias	***grah**-see-ahs*	thank you

grande	*grahn*-day	big
hasta luego	*ahs*-tah-loo-*ay*-goh	see you later
hay	*ah-ee*	there is/there are
el helado	*ehl-lah-doh*	ice cream
la hoja	*lah-oh-hah*	leaf
hola	*oh-la*	hello
el jardín	*ehl-hahr-deen*	garden
la jirafa	*la-hee-rah-fah*	giraffe
la jinete	*lah-hee-nay-tay*	horseback rider
el juguete	*ehl-hoo-gay-tay*	toy
la lección	*lah-lek-see-ohn*	lesson
lento	*lehn-toh*	slow
el león	*ehl-lay-ohn*	lion
ocho	*oh-choh*	eight
la mano	*lah-mah-noh*	hand

me gusta	*meh-**goo**-stah*	I like
me llamo	*meh-**yah**-moh*	my name is
la merienda	*lah-may-ree-**ehn**-dah*	tea time
la muñeca	*lah-moo-**nyay**-kah*	doll
negro	***nay**-groh*	black
no	*noh*	no
nueve	*noo-**ay**-vay*	nine
el oso	*ehl-**oh**-soh*	bear
el osito de pelu-che	*ehl-oh-**see**-toh-day-peh-**loo**-chay*	teddy bear
el pájaro	*ehl-**pah**-hah-roh*	bird
el parque zoo-lógico	*ehl-**pahr**-keh-zoh-**loh**-hee-koh*	zoo
el pastel	*ehl-pahs-**tehl***	cake
el pegaso	*ehl-pay-**gah**-soh*	pegasus

pequeño	*pay-**kay**-nyoh*	small
el perro	*ehl-**pehr**-roh*	dog
el pez	*ehl-pays*	fish
el pie	*ehl-pee-**ay***	foot
la pierna	*lah-pee-**ehr**-nah*	leg
el plato	*ehl-**plah**-toh*	plate
el poni	*ehl-**poh**-nee*	pony
por favor	*pohr-fay-**vohr***	please
la princesa	*lah-prin-**say**-sah*	princess
que tengas un buen viaje	*keh-tehn-gahs-oohn-vee-ah-hay*	have a good trip
rápido	***rah**-pee-doh*	fast
la reina	*lah-**ray**-nah*	queen
rojo	***roh**-hoh*	red
la rosa	*lah-**roh**-sah*	rose

seis	say-ees	six
la sirena	lah-see-**ray**-nah	mermaid
el sombrero	ehl-sohm-**bray**-roh	hat
soy	soy	I am
la tarta	lah-**tahr**-tah	pie
la taza de té	lah-**tahs**-sah-day-tee	tea cup
te gusta	teh-**goo**-stah	you like
tengo	**tayn**-goh	I have
la tetera	lah-tay-**tay**-rah	tea pot
tienes	tee-**ehn**-ehs	you have
el tigre	ehl-**tee**-gray	tiger
tres	trays	three
un/una	oohn/**ooh**-nah	a/an
el unicornio	ehl-oo-nee-**kohr**-nee-oh	unicorn

uno	*oo*-*noh*	one
la vaquera	*lah-vah-**kay**-rah*	cowgirl
veo	***vay**-oh*	I see
verde	***vehrr**-day*	green
ves	*vays*	you see
y	*ee*	and

Memory Game Cards

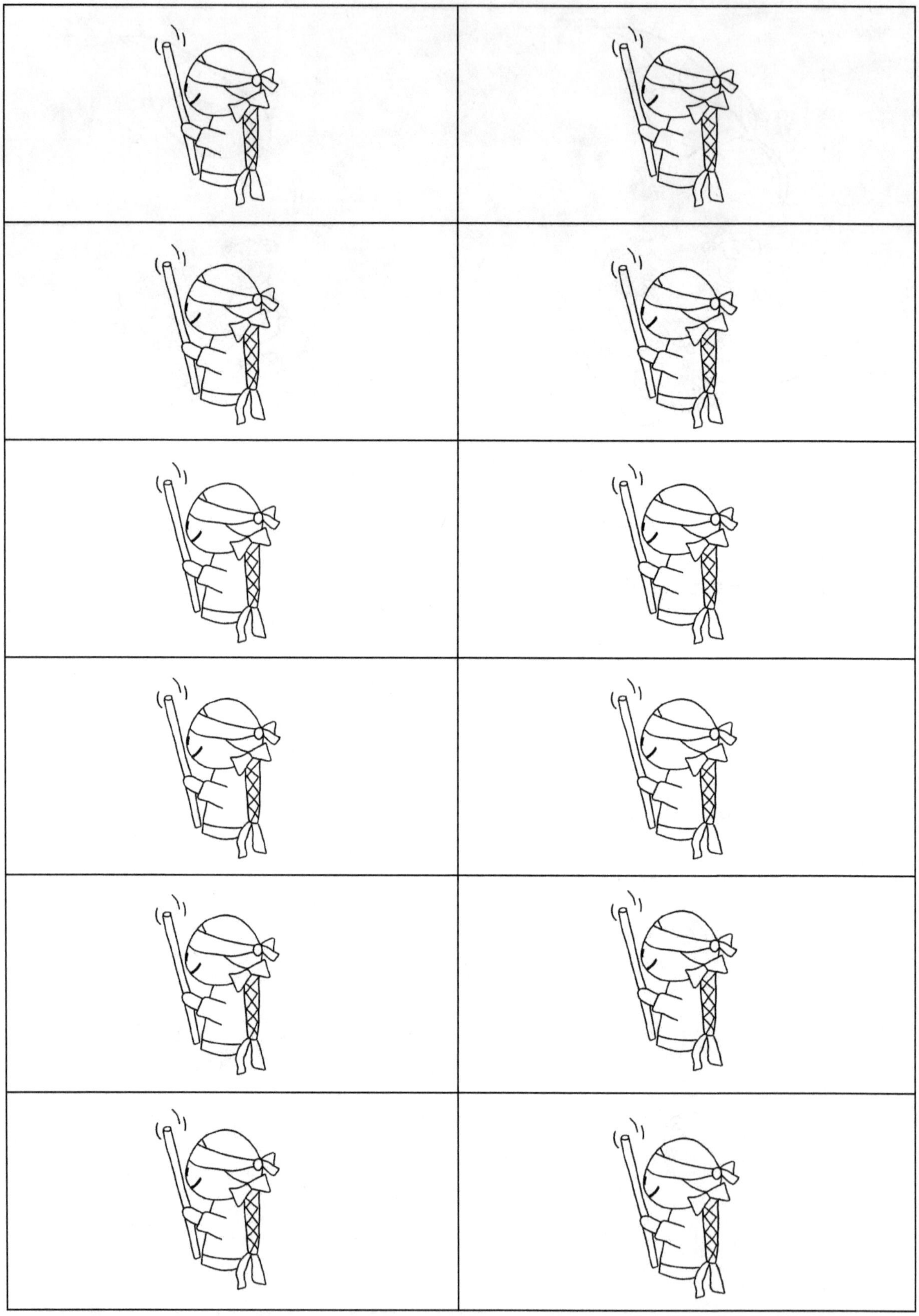

www.ingramcontent.com/pod-product-compliance
Lightning Source LLC
Chambersburg PA
CBHW062107090426
42741CB00015B/3352